Special Occasion Clothes

Jane Bingham

WAYLAND

First published in 2008 by Wayland

Copyright © Wayland 2008

Wayland
338 Euston Road
London NW1 3BH

Wayland
Level 17/207 Kent Street
Sydney NSW 2000

Senior editor: Joyce Bentley
Design: Holly Fullbrook and Rachel Hamdi
Picture researcher: Kathy Lockley

British Library Cataloguing in Publication Data
Bingham, Jane
Celebration clothes. - (Clothes around the world)
1. Costume - Juvenile literature
I. Title
391

ISBN 978 0 7502 5315 4

Picture acknowledgements: AFP/Getty Images: 24, 27; ARISTO/Alamy: 22; Art
Archive/Bibliothèque des Arts Dècoratifs, Paris/Gianni Dagli Orti: 3, 11; Art
Archive/Musée Archéologique, Naples/Gianni Dagli Orti: 8; David Cheskin/PA
Archive/PA Photos: 25; Stephanie Colosanti/Corbis: 21; Comstock/Corbis: 5
Livia Corona/Getty Images: 26; db images/Alamy: 19; Eye Ubiquitous/Corbis: 7;
Chris Fairclough: 28-29; Kevin Fleming/Corbis: 13; Michel Friang/Alamy: 6; Blaine
Harrington III/Corbis: 4; Gavin Hellier/Jon Arnold Images Ltd/Alamy: 14; Israel
Images/Alamy: 18; Kamal Kishore/Reuters/Corbis: 1, 16; Charles & Josette
Lenars/Corbis: 9; Tom Nebbia/Corbis: 12; Profimedia International s.r.o./Alamy: 20;
Phil Schermeister/Corbis: 10; Adreanna Seymour/Getty Images: 23; Sipa Press/Rex
Features: 15; Wishlist: 30; Dan Vander Zwalm/Corbis Sygma: 17

Printed in China

Wayland is a division of Hachette Children's Books,
an Hachette Livre UK company.

Contents

What are special occasion clothes?

When people get together for an important occasion, they like to wear something special. They may wear clothes that are smart and **formal**. Or they may wear something colourful and fun. It's good to wear something different from your everyday clothes when you celebrate a special occasion.

Sometimes people wear **traditional** costumes for a special occasion. Wearing traditional clothes can help to remind you of your history or your religion.

Everyone dresses up for a **carnival** parade! These dancers are parading through the streets on the Caribbean island of Trinidad.

For some occasions, people dress up in fancy dress costumes. They have lots of fun pretending to be someone or something completely different!

Special occasion clothes come in many forms, but they all make you feel different from usual. When you dress up in your special clothes, you know that you are going to do something out of the ordinary.

It Works!

Evening dress
In many countries, men and boys wear evening dress for parties. They dress up in a smart black suit, a white shirt, and a bow tie. Men have been wearing evening dress for 200 years – and it still looks great!

Special clothes around the world

All around the world, people dress up for special occasions. Their costumes vary from country to country. Often the costumes remind people of their country's past.

In Japan, people celebrate the coming of spring. They gather in parks and gardens to admire the cherry blossom. Women and girls wear lightweight robes, decorated with flower patterns. These traditional robes are called yukatas. Men and boys wear short, colourful jackets, known as happi coats.

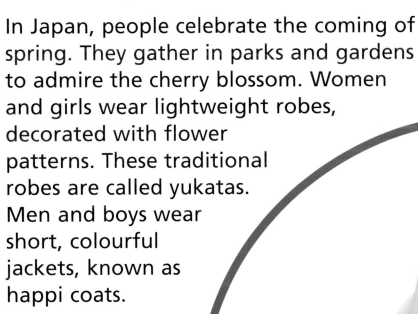

People in Japan celebrate autumn as well as spring. This Japanese girl wears an autumn yukata with a maple leaf pattern.

The people of Wales celebrate Saint David's day. They sing songs and recite poems about their **patron saint**. On Saint David's day, some women and girls dress in their national costume. They wear a long skirt, a shawl around their shoulders, and a tall black hat.

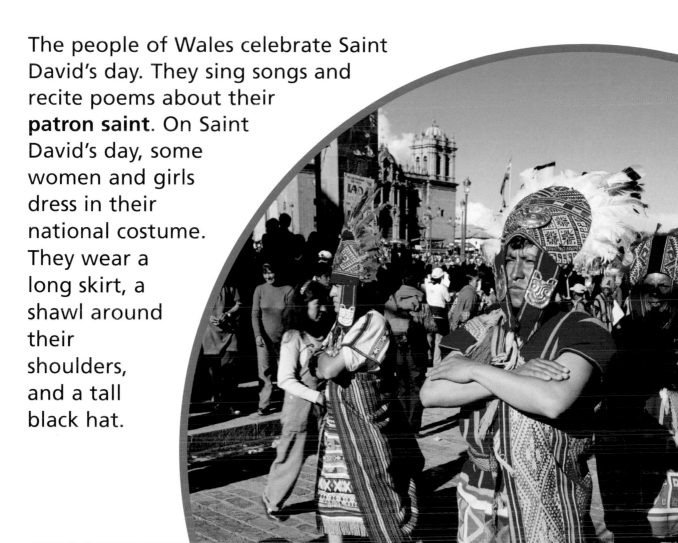

Flashback

Remembering the Incas
The Inca **civilization** in Peru came to an end 500 years ago. But the Incas are not forgotten. Every year the people of Peru hold a Festival of the Sun. At this festival, people dress in the colourful costumes of their ancestors.

The history of special clothes

People have always dressed up for special occasions. In **prehistoric times**, hunters held dances before they set out to hunt. They painted patterns on their bodies and wore necklaces made from bones and seeds. The leader of the dance wore a headdress made from deer's antlers.

In Roman times, wealthy people dressed up in their finest clothes for a banquet.

In ancient Egypt, wealthy people held parties. All the guests dressed in fine linen robes, with lots of jewellery. Men and women wore bracelets and rings, and wide necklaces that looked like collars. Women had black wigs and dramatic eye make-up.

Roman emperors held grand banquets with many courses. Male guests wore togas – a length of woollen cloth wrapped around the body and draped over one shoulder. Women had long dresses, known as stolas, and colourful shawls. They also wore lots of jewellery made from gold and precious stones.

Weird and Wonderful

Curious cones
When the guests arrived at an Egyptian party, servants placed cones of perfumed fat on their heads. During the evening, the cones melted. The melted fat kept the guests cool, and made them smell good too!

By the 1200s, there were many tribes of Native Americans living in North America. Tribes held powwows, when all their members came together to sing and dance. Native American dancers wore tall feather headdresses and costumes made from leather and fur.

In the 1800s, rich people in Europe loved to go to balls. Women wore ball gowns made from velvet, silk or satin. Men wore tight-fitting trousers and **tailcoats**, and had shirts with ruffles down the front.

Some Native Americans still hold powwows. These members of the Chippewa people still wear traditional costumes for their powwow.

Rock-and-roll parties were very popular in the 1950s. They were a chance for young people to dance together. The girls wore very wide skirts that twirled around when they danced. The boys wore leather jackets and tight denim jeans.

Painful dresses
In the 1700s, it was the fashion for women to wear dresses with very tiny waists. When they tried to dance, they found it hard to breathe and they often fainted. By the 1800s, a looser style of dress had developed. This meant that women could dance more easily.

A painting of a ball in the early 1800s. The men wear elegant evening dress, and the women have loose-fitting ball gowns.

What are special clothes made from?

The earliest celebration clothes were made from natural materials. People made headdresses and clothes from leather, fur and feathers. They wore skirts made from dried grass and carved masks from wood. They also created necklaces from shells, bones and seeds.

This dancer comes from the island of Tahiti. Her costume is made from dried grass, beads and flowers.

Flowers play an important part in clothes for special occasions. In the South Sea Islands, dancers wear flower garlands round their necks. In some countries, people welcome the spring by performing dances and wearing flower garlands in their hair.

Feathers make great celebration clothes. They come in many colours, and they can have different meanings. In some Native American headdresses, a feather with a red dot shows that the wearer has killed an enemy.

Today, feathers are dyed bright colours and made into long scarves, called feather boas. Women often wear a feather boa as part of a party outfit.

Weird and Wonderful

Magic feathers
The Aztec people lived in Mexico around 1400 CE. For their celebrations, they wore headdresses with bright green feathers. The feathers came from the Quetzalcoatl bird, which the Aztecs worshipped as a god. They believed its feathers had magic powers.

Today, descendants of the Aztecs sometimes dress up in magnificent headdresses, like the ones their **ancestors** wore.

In some parts of Africa, people still carve masks from wood. They create dramatic faces that look like spirits and animals. Some masks are decorated with feathers, grasses or shells. People wear these masks to perform traditional dances.

Party clothes can be made from really special materials, such as velvet, silk or satin. These materials are too expensive to wear everyday, but they look great for a party.

These members of the West African Dogon tribe are wearing animal masks for a traditional dance.

People often like to wear lots of jewellery for parties. Rich women sometimes wear a necklace or a tiara made from diamonds. But party jewellery does not need to be expensive. Many people choose jewellery just because it looks fun. They may wear a colourful necklace made from glass, wood or plastic.

Flashback

Masks past and present

When you wear a mask, you can forget your usual self, and take on a completely different **role**. In the past, masks were usually made from wood, but most modern masks are made from plastic or card.

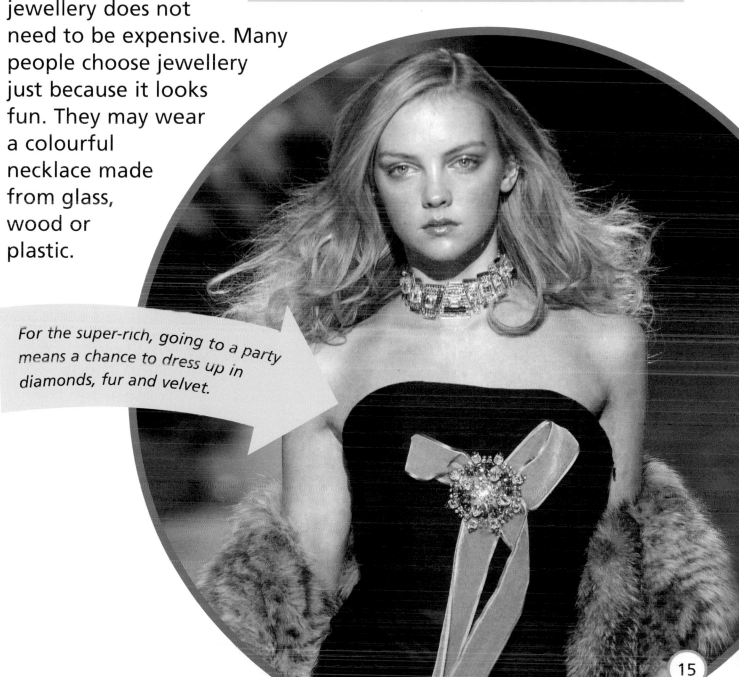

For the super-rich, going to a party means a chance to dress up in diamonds, fur and velvet.

Clothes for religious festivals

People often wear special costumes for religious festivals. These traditional clothes help them to remember the history of their religion.

Members of the **Sikh** religion have a festival called Hola Mohalla. At this festival Sikh men dress as warriors. They wear colourful robes and **turbans** and they carry long, curved swords. The costumes help them remember the time when Sikhs fought to defend their religion.

Sikhs celebrating Hola Mohalla. The man in the very large turban belongs to a special group of 'holy warriors' in the Sikh religion.

In Sweden, **Christians** celebrate Saint Lucia's day. They remember how Saint Lucia stayed unharmed, even when she was surrounded by fire. Girls in long white dresses sing songs to the saint. They wear special headdresses with holders for lighted candles.

It Doesn't Work!

Hair on fire

In the past, Swedish girls wore real candles on Saint Lucia's day. This was very dangerous, and some girls' hair caught on fire. Now girls still wear headdresses with candles, but the candles have lights worked by batteries.

These children are celebrating the Jewish festival of Purim. They are all dressed as followers of the wicked Haman.

Jewish children remember their people's past at the festival of Purim. They dress up in costumes and masks to tell an exciting story from the Bible. The story tells how Queen Esther and her people stood up to their enemy, Haman.

It Works!

Bracelets for brothers

Some festival clothes help people to think about something important. In the **Hindu** festival of Raksha Bandhan, a sister ties a bracelet round her brother's wrist. Afterwards, the bracelet stays on the boy's wrist. It reminds him of his close link with his sister.

On the island of Sri Lanka, **Buddhists** hold the Festival of the Tooth. Once a year, an enormous crowd marches to the temple where a holy tooth is kept. Flag bearers wear white costumes with scarlet sashes, and dancers wear monkey masks. The guardians of the tooth ride on elephants and wear sparkling costumes covered with jewels. The parade is full of colour, but the richest costumes of all are worn by the elephants!

Dancers in elaborate costumes take part in the Festval of the Tooth.

Clothes for carnivals

Carnivals are celebrations that everyone can take part in. They are held in the streets and include lively music and dancing. People often wear fancy dress and masks for carnivals.

There are carnivals all over the world, but the biggest of all is the Rio Carnival. It is held in the city of Rio de Janeiro, in Brazil. The Rio Carnival is famous for its amazing costume parades. In the parades, people forget their everyday lives. Poor people dress as princes and princesses, men dress as women, and rich people sometimes pretend to be poor.

At the Rio Carnival, people compete to see who can have the most astonishing costume.

The city of Cologne in Germany has a very large fancy dress parade. The parade is led by three figures from fairy tales – the prince, the maiden, and the peasant.

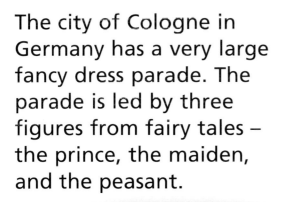

A group of costumed characters at the Venice Carnival. The King and Queen of Hearts are dressed in red.

Wedding clothes

All over the world, people wear special clothes for weddings. Most wedding clothes have a very long history.

In Britain and America, it is traditional for the bride to wear a long white dress. Sometimes the bride also has a veil over her face. The **groom** usually wears a suit. In very formal weddings, he wears a tailcoat and a top hat.

This bride is carrying a posy of flowers and the bridesmaids are too. The groom wears a flower on his jacket.

In a Hindu wedding, the bride wears a sari made from silk and her hair is covered with a veil. The groom usually wears a long silk coat over a tunic and trousers.

During the wedding ceremony, the bride and groom have garlands of flowers placed around their necks. They also have their clothes knotted together to show that they are joined as a couple.

Hindu brides usually wear red because the colour red symbolizes happiness.

Clothes for New Year

Many people celebrate the start of the New Year. Some dress up in party clothes and others wear fancy dress. In China and Scotland, people often wear traditional clothes to welcome the New Year.

New Year is a very important time for Chinese families. Some people dress up in dragon costumes and parade through the streets. Others wear traditional Chinese dress, to remind them of their ancestors. Most people try to wear something red, because red is seen as a lucky colour.

These girls are wearing traditional Chinese dress for their New Year celebrations.

In Scotland, New Year is known as Hogmanay. At Hogmanay, most Scottish people wear their traditional costumes and many of them perform Scottish dances. Men wear a kilt with a short jacket and knee-length socks. Women wear dresses with tartan sashes.

It Works!

Tartan history

Scottish kilts don't just look good. They also have special meanings. Each family group, or clan, has its own tartan with its own special colours and patterns. Wearing a special tartan helps people to remember their family history.

At Hogmanay parties, everyone loves to wear tartan, but not all the costumes are traditional.

Hallowe'en clothes

Hallowe'en is celebrated on the night of October 31st. In the past, people believed that this was the night when ghosts roamed the earth. Today, most people see Hallowe'en as a chance to dress up and have fun.

At Hallowe'en, children dress up as scary characters and visit local houses. The most popular characters are witches, **vampires**, skeletons and ghosts.

Some Mexicans wear costumes and masks to mark the Day of the Dead on November 1st.

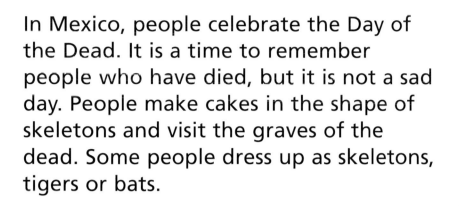

In Mexico, people celebrate the Day of the Dead. It is a time to remember people who have died, but it is not a sad day. People make cakes in the shape of skeletons and visit the graves of the dead. Some people dress up as skeletons, tigers or bats.

Weird and Wonderful

Cartoon costumes
Recently, people in Japan have started to celebrate Hallowe'en. Some of them wear traditional Hallowe'en costumes, but many others dress as cartoon characters. Children often wear Manga or Pokemon costumes.

Make your own carnival mask

Many people wear masks at carnival time. They dress up as amazing creatures and parade through the streets. This colourful mask is fun to wear at parties. When you put it on, you can pretend to be a carnival clown!

Figure 1

1. On the coloured card, draw and cut out the shape shown here. Check that it fits over your nose. Cut out holes for eyes.

Figure 2

2. Cut out shapes from some different coloured card and glue them on to the mask as decoration. Staple rik rak round the edges.

28

3. Cut out a tall triangle from a piece of folded card. Cut a small slit at the bottom of the triangle. Then fold up the two edges to make tabs.

Figure 3

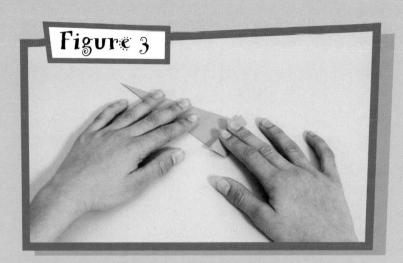

4. Stick double-sided tape on to each tab and stick the tabs to the back of the mask so that the nose sticks out.

Figure 4

Punch a hole on either side of the mask. Tie a thread to each side and fasten the threads behind your head. Now you can get into the carnival mood!

Dress-up box

5-minute Hallowe'en ghost

Children often dress up as ghosts at Hallowe'en. To make your own ghost costume, you will need an old white sheet, some scissors and a thick marker pen.

Try to find some white clothes to wear under your costume. If you wear a hairband or a hat over your costume, it will help to hold it more firmly in place.

1. Put the sheet over your head and ask an adult to draw two large circles where your eyes are.

2. Also ask the adult to mark some points on the sheet just above your ankles. (This will show how much the sheet needs to be shortened.)

3. Take off the sheet, and ask your adult helper to cut out the eyeholes. Also ask your helper to cut off the bottom of the sheet in a ragged line.

4. Use the marker pen to colour round the eyeholes. Then add a ghostly mouth.

5. Put the sheet back on, and start to make ghostly noises!

Glossary

ancestors – people in your family who lived a long time ago

Buddhists – people who follow the teachings of the Lord Buddha. The religion of Buddhism is practised mainly in Asia.

carnival – a celebration in the streets. Some carnivals are part of a religious festival.

Christians – people who follow the teachings of Jesus Christ

civilization – a very well-organized group of people, with their own language and customs

formal – smart and not casual

groom – a man who is about to get married, or has just been married

Hindu – belonging to the religion of Hinduism, the main religion of India. Hindus worship many gods.

Jewish – belonging to the religion of Judaism, which began in Israel. Jews believe in a single god and have the Old Testament of the Bible as their holy book.

patron saint – a saint who is believed to look after a particular country

prehistoric times – a period of time thousands of years ago, before history was written down

rock-and-roll – a kind of dance music with a strong beat and a simple tune

role – a part that you play, especially when you are acting in the theatre

Sikh – belonging to the religion of Sikhism, which began in India. Sikhs believe in a single god.

tailcoat – a smart coat with two long tails at the back

traditional – used or worn in the same way for hundreds of years

turban – a headdress made from a long cloth wound around the head

vampire – a creature in folk tales and horror stories that is supposed to suck human blood

Index

Photos or pictures are shown below in bold, **like this**.